Bonnie Scotland

Within this book is a selection of images covering some of Scotland's most picturesque scenery. Accepting that we cannot incorporate all of Scotland into one book, we have endeavoured to select over 200 images of the most popular and best recognised destinations which best portray the diversity of the Scottish landscape.

Photography by
Graeme Wallace & Derek Wallace

Bonnie Scotland

INTRODUCTION

Welcome to a land of intrigue, diversity, history, colour, and charm. We hope this book will provide you with an informative introduction to Scotland. Either acting as a lasting reminder of your visit, or encouraging you to come and explore some of Scotland's appeal for yourself.

Brothers Graeme and Derek Wallace were born in Fraserburgh, Scotland, and have spent many years photographing their home country. Recognised landscape photographers, their work has appeared in numerous travel publications including a similar format book of the Canadian Rockies.

Featured within these pages are many of Scotland's great castles. These range from ruins to majestic buildings which are just as complete today as they were when first built. Spanning some 7 centuries dating from as early as the 11th Century, many were built as strongholds to protect their occupants and belongings from attacks by invading enemies. Others have been built as family or Clan homes, some having very ornate finishes with towers and turrets which seem to provide very little in the way of defence but exude their owners' wealth. In stark contrast to its warring history, the rolling heather clad mountains, peaceful glens, clear burns and tranquil lochs serve to calm the spirit. Now however, as you explore this colourful landscape the castles blend into the surroundings and provide a more romantic and thought provoking experience to visitors.

With such charming landscape it's no surprise that many an artist has drawn inspiration from their home surroundings. Robert Burns is certainly the most famous, but there have been plenty of others such as Sir Walter Scott, Robert Louis Stevenson, Reverend John Thomson, Charles Rennie Mackintosh and Hugh MacDiarmid to name just a few. Visiting artists also came to interpret the dramatic and ever changing light. JMW Turner visited Sir Walter Scott at his home in Abbotsford in July 1831 and made several engravings, such as the "View of River Tweed and Dryburgh Abbey" that was published in 1832.

Although Scotland has a reputation for unpredictable weather there are many positive attributes to counterbalance this fact. The instantly recognisable green and lush landscape for one is of course a direct result of the high yearly rainfall. Another positive aspect is the many types of natural spring water, each having its own unique qualities which in turn, plays a direct and vital part in the manufacture of Scotland's most well renowned export, namely Malt Whisky. And if that isn't a good enough reason on its own, the high annual rainfall also provides much of the country's power, in the form of hydro electricity. Finally the changing weather provides variable lighting conditions which helps photographers produce their creative and unique pictures.

Scotland's geography spans from the lowlands and progresses to the rolling hills of the southern uplands where much of the country's agriculture takes place. Further north, you cannot escape the 'classic' image of Scotland; that of the mountains, lochs and glens. Visitors are rewarded with a unique and inspiring range of dramatic views whichever season. Beyond the mainland are of course the islands, many of which are inhabited by small crofting and fishing communities.

ACKNOWLEDGMENTS

Photography by **Graeme Wallace & Derek Wallace**
Edited by **James Tims**
Designed by **Kevin Jeffery**
Reprographics by **L.C. Reprographics**
Printed by **Printer Trento, Italy**

Published by
GW Publishing
PO Box 6091, Thatcham, Berks, RG19 8XZ.
Tel: +44 (0)1635 268080

First Published 2001
Revised 2005

© Copyright GW Publishing
Photographs © Copyright Graeme Wallace & Derek Wallace

Great care has been taken to ensure the accuracy of the information in this book, however we will not be held liable for any inaccuracy.

ISBN 09535397 9 2

To order other publications visit www.gwpublishing.com

Appreciating the limitations of reproducing a panoramic vista to the size of a print, both Graeme and Derek Wallace continually endeavour to incorporate a sense of depth and life into their work while photographing this tranquil land. One aspect that can never be captured by pictures, are the sounds of Scotland, from the peaceful ripple of the burns and lapping loch shores, to the eerie sound of the bagpipes played within the mountains and castles. Nevertheless we hope the beautiful and evocative images in this book will help to create a memorable visual image of the total Scottish experience.

Pictured above, Highland Cow, native breed of Scotland.

Pictured opposite, Corgarff Castle

Pictured page 1, Eilean Donan Castle, backdrop to a Scottish Piper.

Pictured page 2, Edinburgh Castle, located in Scotland's capital.

Pictured page 4, Ben Nevis, the highest mountain in Scotland and Great Britain 4,406 ft (1344 m).

Front Cover, Duart Castle.   Back Cover, Castle Stalker.

Inside Front Cover, Wallace Dress Tartan.   Inside Back Cover, Wallace Hunting Tartan.

Bonnie
Scotland

Scotland

80 kms
50 miles

ATLANTIC OCEAN

The numbers on this map refer to the page numbers on page 9.

Bonnie Scotland

Contents

Border Abbeys

Four magnificent Abbeys situated along the border 13 miles apart in a triangular arrangement were founded by King David of Scotland between 1128 and 1150. Although a turbulent past has caused the ruin of these Gothic abbeys, they are still intact enough to reflect the grandeur and dominance they once exuded.

Jedburgh Abbey

BELOW/RIGHT Founded in 1138 the abbey has been destroyed and rebuilt eight times, yet despite this its early Gothic arches are remarkably preserved. In fact, the most intact of the four border abbeys, the main tower and imposing walls are a reminder of the scale of this influential building.

Kelso Abbey

LEFT The first of the four Border abbeys and at one time the greatest, it was founded in 1128. However with it being in the path of successive English invading armies it has suffered more than the others and is now the most ruined.

11

Dryburgh Abbey

ABOVE *Built in a remote and tranquil setting along the River Tweed, it was the last of the four Border abbeys to be founded, in 1150. While its turbulent past is evident, it now provides a peaceful location for the grave of Sir Walter Scott.*

Dryburgh
Abbey

Melrose Abbey

BELOW Founded in 1136 it has been sacked
many times with today's ruin dating back
to the 15th century. A heart believed to be
that of Robert the Bruce is buried here.

Abbotsford House

<small>INSET</small> *The home of Sir Walter Scott which he built in 1812 overlooking the River Tweed. Scott was a collector of armoury and his house displays an impressive array of weapons; including Rob Roy's gun whom he romanticised in a novel of the same name.*

From the hills overlooking Dryburgh Abbey, and the River Tweed the Eildon Hills can be seen in the distance. Known as Scott's View this is where the novelist would often look out and contemplate.

Floors Castle

Situated along the River Tweed and built
in the 1720's for the Dukes of Roxburghe,
it is the largest inhabited castle in Scotland
and still home to the present Duke and
Duchess. The turrets are more ornamental
than defensive and the building more a
palace than a castle.

Thirlestane Castle - Lauder

INSET Affectionately called Scotland's fairy
tale castle, it is one of the seven Great
Houses of Scotland, and was the ancient
seat of the earls and Duke of Lauderdale.
It's origins lie in the 13th Century, but
was rebuilt in 1590, then extended in both
1670 and 1840.

Preston Mill

LEFT *This 18th century red pantile roofed mill is still mechanically intact, and is one of Scotland's oldest working water driven mills for grinding oatmeal.*

Tantallon Castle

ABOVE *Standing on a rugged cliff top overlooking the Firth of Forth, the 14th century castle was a formidable fortress until it fell in 1651 to Cromwell. Its thick 50ft (15m) high wall formed part of the living area and incorporates numerous stairways to the turrets along the top of the wall.*

Edinburgh

Scotland's capital since 1124 when the throne moved from Dunfermline to Edinburgh. Its castle stands as sentry over the whole city which can be divided into two by the main road through the city - Princes Street. To the east of the castle is the Georgian New Town, built to relieve the squalor and rancid stench of the Old Town which led down from the Castle to Holyrood Palace. Now however, the squalor and stench has gone and the Royal Mile of the Old Town is a gem of intriguing, and beautifully restored buildings. It is also the area where The Edinburgh Festival takes place. The annual cultural and arts festival lights up the streets day and night, with a vibrant array of sounds and colourful performers.

Edinburgh Castle

With its obvious formidable position, the volcanic rocky hill on which Edinburgh Castle is built has been used as a fortification site for almost 2000 years. Along with Mons Meg, a huge 15th century cannon, the castle houses the Scottish Crown Jewels and the Stone of Destiny. The 11th century chapel within the walls is the oldest part of the castle and in fact the oldest building in Edinburgh. Being the principal building in the capital city the castle witnessed many battles and control passed between the Scots and the English many times.

The motto of the Royal Arms of Scotland as written above the Castle entrance is "Nemo Me Impune Lacessit" translated "if you hit me we'll hit you back harder".

War Memorial

BELOW Erected to commemorate the soldiers who fought and died for Britain in the 1899 Boer War and World War II.

Edinburgh

Military Tattoo

ABOVE *A piper of The First Royal Tank Regiment joins the Massed Pipes and Drums at the 50th Tattoo.*

RIGHT *A member of The Mounted Band of the Life Guards plays the post horn supported by The Band of the Royal Lancers, The Band of the Dragoon Guards, The Band of the Hussars and Light Dragoons and The Royal Tank Regiment Cambrai Band.*

LEFT *The castle is the centre for the month long Military Tattoo and the annual Hogmanay celebrations on New Years Eve.*

Edinburgh

John Knox House

BELOW *A beautifully restored medieval house dating from 1490, it is the oldest dwelling house in the city. The jettied first floor overhanging the street to increase floor space was common amongst buildings in this period. Dedicated to the memory of John Knox, a devout Presbyterian reformer and fierce critic of Mary Queen of Scots.*

Canongate Tolbooth

RIGHT *The clock tower Tolbooth was the administrative centre for people who lived and worked in the vicinity of Edinburgh in the 18th century and now serves as the Peoples Story Museum, telling the story of the poverty, squalor and hard-working conditions of these people.*

24

Edinburgh

The Palace of Holyroodhouse

The Queens Official residence in Scotland, situated at the eastern end of the Royal Mile. Founded by Scots' king David 1 in 1128 it has been rebuilt on numerous occasions, with the existing building largely dating from the 1670's. Home to Mary, Queen of Scots' in 1561-67, this Baroque palace has seen murder, betrayal and courage.

Scott Monument - Edinburgh

INSET *Towering above Princes Street Gardens, 287 steps take you to the top of the Gothic spire monument dedicated to Sir Walter Scott.*

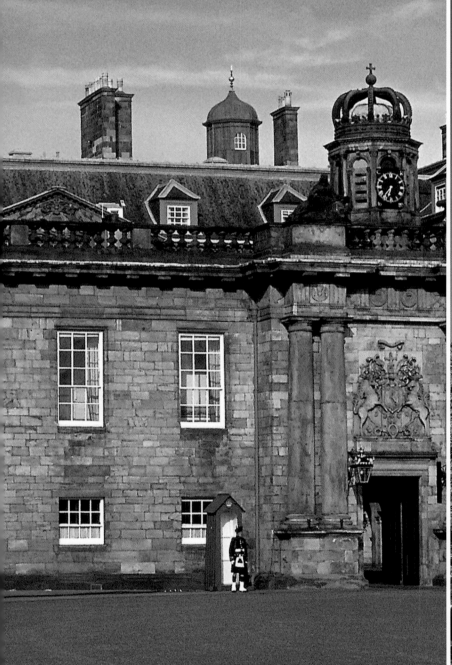

Edinburgh

The Georgian House, No.7 Charlotte Square

LEFT To relieve the overcrowding and squalor in Edinburgh's old town an elegant "New Town" was planned and building started in 1770. Charlotte Square is a fine example of the Georgian architect James Craig's orderly geometric plan.

Royal Botanic Garden Edinburgh

BELOW Scotlands national botanic garden encompasses more than 70 acres of landscaped grounds. Edinburgh's Royal Botanic Garden boasts a magnificent rock garden, exotic plants from around the world and ten glasshouses, including the tallest Palm House in Britain.

Linlithgow Palace
Built in 1425 overlooking Linlithgow Loch, this is where Mary Queen of Scots was born in 1542. It was used as a court but was abandoned in 1745 after a dreadful fire.

Edinburgh - National Gallery

Situated on a mound where once stood
Loch Nor, and which is now Princes
Street Gardens, the neo-Classical
columned National Gallery of Scotland
contains a superb collection of art from
the Renaissance to the post-Impressionist
period.

Edinburgh Castle

The Castle is without doubt Edinburgh's, if not Scotland's most powerful landmark. The castle as seen today has been built, modified and extended through the ages since the 13th century. It has been fought over and changed hands between the English and Scots many times until the creation of the United Kingdom in 1717.

Royal Yacht Britannia

Launched in 1953 the Royal Yacht Britannia provided an escape and sanctuary for the Royal Family, however after one million miles and nearly 1,000 official voyages it was decommissioned in 1997. Now permanently moored along side the Ocean Terminal in Leith, it is a floating museum offering a nostalgic glimpse into the esteemed world of the Royal Family.

Traquair House -
Innerleithen

BELOW A refuge for Mary Queen of Scots
and later, Prince Charles Edward Stuart
(Bonnie Prince Charlie). Originally built in
the 12th century and largely rebuilt/extended
in 1680. It is the oldest continuously
inhabited house in Scotland. In the 18th
century the wrought iron gates were closed
and it was decreed that they should not re-
open until a Stuart king sits on the British
throne again.

Neidpath Castle - Peebles

RIGHT Erected in the 14th century on the
steep rocky banks of a deep valley above
the River Tweed. The 11ft (3m) thick
walls suffered during an attack by
Cromwellian forces in 1650. The castle
was later 'modernised' at the end of the
17th century, but part of the west wing
fell away in the early 19th century.

New Lanark Village

LEFT *Nominated a UNESCO World Heritage Site, New Lanark is situated alongside the River Clyde in a densely wooded gorge. Founded in 1785 by David Dale as a revolutionary industrial settlement, it had four cotton mills by 1820, and a population of over 2,500. Using profits to improve the benefits and conditions of the workers, Robert Owen made New Lanark famous as a model community.*

Gretna Green - Old Blacksmiths Shop

ABOVE *Up until 1940 eloping couples from England would cross the border to marry here in Scotland where no parental consent was needed. A witnessed declaration was all that was required.*

Caerlaverock Castle

Built c.1280 this triangular castle, the only one in Britain, with its moat and substantial twin drum-tower gatehouse is a wonderful example of a medieval fortification and provides a graphic reminder of the cross border struggle between Scotland and England.

Drumlanrig Castle

ABOVE *Set on a mound near the River Nith and built with pink sandstone, this 17th century palace with its four corner towers was built to replace the former Douglas stronghold of Sanquhar Castle.*

Threave Garden

64 acres of peaceful and rolling gardens, Threave is best known for its spectacular collection of almost 200 varieties of daffodil.

**Threave Castle,
near Castle Douglas**

*Ring the bell and a boatman will row
across and take you to a medieval
harbour on an island in the River Dee,
and to Archibald the Grim's 14th century
castle. This was the stronghold of the
Black Douglases who would mercilessly
pillage the neighbouring homesteads until
they were overthrown in 1455.*

New Abbey Corn Mill

BELOW Driven by the great wheel outside, this 18th century water mill was used to produce oatmeal. Now renovated, it is one of only a few historic mills which remain in working order.

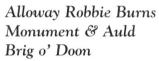

Alloway Robbie Burns Monument & Auld Brig o' Doon

Acclaimed as Scotland's greatest literary influence, Robert Burns was born January 25th 1759 in Alloway, in the small white washed, thatched roofed cottage now part of the Burns National Heritage Park. Just below the Grecian style monument erected to Burns in 1823 is the 17th century Auld Brig o' Doon. A picturesque reminder of one of his most famous poems about Tam o' Shanter who had a tendency to have a "wee dram too many".

Brodick Castle

Overlooking the Brodick Bay on the island of Arran, Brodick Castle was built by the Crown from red sandstone on the site of a Viking fortress. Part of the castle dates back to the 13th century.

Culzean Castle-Ayr

A coastal 18th century castle south of Ayr. Although the need for castles had diminished by the 18th century, this Italianate style castle incorporated a defensive appearance, while Robert Adam's interior is noted as one of the finest in Scotland.

Glasgow

City Chambers

ABOVE Opened in 1888 by Queen Victoria at the head of George Square, the magnificent Victorian façade of the City Chambers were modelled on the Italian Renaissance style.

The Clyde Auditorium

BELOW *Designed by Sir Norman Foster and affectionately known as the "Armadillo", the auditorium is situated alongside the River Clyde. Built as an expansion of the Scottish Exhibition and Conference Centre, it was completed in September 1997, and boasts over 240,000 square feet (22,000 sq m) of floor space.*

Glasgow Cathedral

BELOW *The cathedral is the only building to remain from the old medieval town of Glasgow. Founded by Glasgow's patron St Mungo in the 6th century, this imposing Gothic cathedral was built on the site of an earlier church dating back to the 1st century, and has survived far better than the abbeys in South East Scotland.*

Glasgow

Art Gallery

BELOW *Situated in the leafy Kelvingrove Park, this splendid red sandstone Victorian mansion houses Glasgow's principal art gallery and museum.*

Loch Lomond

Loch Lomond is the largest freshwater loch in Scotland. A chain of Islands stretches across the loch and lie on the fault line which marks the beginning of the Highlands.

Ben Lomond

Dominating the "bonnie banks" of Loch Lomond, at 3,195ft (974m) Ben Lomond is Scotland's most southerly Munro and provides an excellent vantage point to view the loch and surrounding hills.

53

Mount Stuart House - Isle of Bute

ABOVE *A magnificent Victorian house, Mt Stuart House was built within beautiful wooded surroundings and was the first residence in Scotland to be lit by electricity*

Rothesay Castle - Bute

RIGHT *An early 13th century medieval circular castle built by the Stewart clan on this "holiday" island. It is believed that an earlier castle stood on the moated site on which the present partly-ruined castle stands.*

Inveraray Castle

RIGHT Built from locally quarried chloritic schist in the 18th century, Inveraray Castle replaced a 15th century fortified keep. It is the headquarters of Clan Campbell and home of the Duke and Duchess of Argyll whose ancestors moved from Loch Awe in the 15th Century.

Kilchurn Castle - Loch Awe

BELOW Kilchurn castle was built on a rock at the head of Loch Awe in 1440 by the Clan Campbell and remained their stronghold until 1740. Loch Awe is the longest freshwater loch in Scotland.

Carraig Fhada Lighthouse

RIGHT *The coast of Islay was notoriously dangerous with over 250 wrecks and strandings being recorded around its shores. The waters approaching Port Ellen are visibly treacherous with many large rocks jutting out into the sea for 3 to 4 miles. The Carraig Fhada Lighthouse was built in 1832 marking a channel allowing large vessels to enter Port Ellen in safety. The lighthouse has now been converted to run on solar power.*

Bowmore Church

ABOVE *Following the Highland clearances, the town of Bowmore was built in 1768 to be the Islands capital. The circular 'round church' at the top of the hill was built round to ensure the Devil and his evil spirits had no corner to hide.*

Portnahaven

ABOVE *Islay's most westerly and remote village clinging to the Rhinns Peninsula. The village is so remote and peaceful that seals happily sit out on the rocks within the harbour.*

Lagavulin Distillery

RIGHT *Lagavulin Distillery sits between Laphroag and Ardbeg Distilleries, just 3 miles apart. Having survived the ups and downs of whisky consumption over the centuries, the fact that all three are still in production is an accolade for the unique heavily peated style of whisky produced from these distilleries.*

Oban from McCaig's Tower

Overlooking the beautiful bay of Oban is Oban distillery and above it the McCaigs Tower. The circular tower was built in Victorian times by John Stuart McCaig. Oban is a busy gateway to the isle of Mull.
INSET *Lynn of Lorne*

Duart Castle - Mull

Defended by sea on three sides, imposing Duart Castle guards the sound of Mull. Dating from the 13th century, Duart Castle was built by the Macleans, and is currently home to the Chief of the Clan. It is one of the oldest inhabited castles in Scotland.

Tobermory - Mull

INSET The colourful fishing harbour on the north of the Island of Mull is also home to the distillery and single malt named after the village.

Castle Stalker, Loch Linnhe

A classic 15th century tower house set on Hunter's Island, guarding the mouth of Loch Linnhe where it meets the Sound of Shuna. In addition to being used for defensive purposes it was also a base from where King James IV and the 2nd chief of Clan Stewart - Duncan would go hunting. (private castle - not open to the public)

Loch Linnhe

Black Mount, Rannoch Moor

Once a huge ice field, Rannoch Moor has an average of 100 inches of rain per year. This makes it an uninhabitable desolate bog. Yet while bleak for many days of the year, it becomes highly evocative as the sun breaks through to illuminate and cast shadows across the moorland and distant peaks making it a haven for photographers and artists striving to capture its unique mood.

Three Sisters, Glencoe

Three peaks of Bidean nam Bian form the Three Sisters of Glen Coe. Standing over the deep gorge through which runs the River Coe, this narrow glen was the scene of the infamous and tragic massacre of members of the MacDonald clan in 1692.

71

Buachaille Etive Mor
Gaelic for "The Great Shepherd of Etive"
at 3,343ft (1,019 m), the mountain
stands guard over the pass from Rannoch
Moor to Glen Coe.

Red Deer
INSET Young red deer stag braves a blizzard
on Rannoch Moor.

Falls of Dochart, Killin

LEFT *Crashing over and through rugged rocks and boulders on its way to Loch Tay, the turbulent water of the River Dochart at Killin are spectacular to witness all year round, and particularly so in the autumn.*

Loch Lubnaig

ABOVE *Close by the Trossachs, Loch Lubnaig provides stunning views toward Scotland's "Kyber Pass" and the mountains of the Highlands.*

Drummond Castle Gardens

RIGHT *These impeccably laid out gardens were remodelled in the early 1950's. Some of the plants were retained including the copper beech trees planted in 1842 by Queen Victoria.*

Glenturret Distillery

LEFT Dating from 1775, the Glenturret Distillery is the oldest distillery in Scotland still in production and was one of the first to open its doors to the public in 1980. Despite being one of the smallest distilleries in Scotland, it has a restaurant and hi-tech visitor exhibition resulting in it being a popular tourist destination.

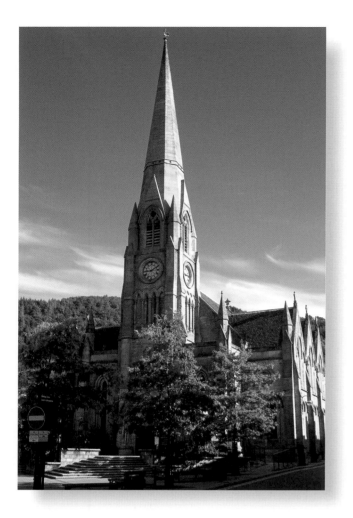

Rob Roy Centre

LEFT *The Trossachs are widely recognised as Rob Roy Country, home to Scotland's most notorious outlaw. The former Callander church is now a visitors centre and provides an excellent place to start a tour of the area and to determine whether Rob Roy MacGregor was an outlaw or a folk hero!*

Loch Achray - Ben Venue

Strictly speaking the area known as the Trossachs only includes the rough hilly region between Loch Achray and Loch Katrine. The tallest mountain in the Trossachs - Ben Venue can be seen lit by the early morning sun beyond Loch Achray.

Falls of Leny

RIGHT Just north of Callander a short trail leads along a steep gorge to the Falls of Leny where the River Leny thunders through a narrow boulder strewn pass.

Loch Katrine - Trossachs

Looking down from Ben A'an, it is easy to see why Loch Katrine was the inspiration for and romanticised by Sir Walter Scott's poem "The Lady of the Lake".

Loch Katrine

Loch Katrine lies in the very heart of the Trossachs, the area which has become synonymous with Rob Roy leader of the MacGregor clan who was born here in 1671.

Loch Ard

ABOVE *Just beyond the village of Aberfoyle lies peaceful Loch Ard on the road to the head of Loch Katrine and the eastern shores of Loch Lomond.*

Doune Castle

Incorporating two towers connected by the great hall, Doune Castle was built for the Regent Albany in the 14th century. One of the finest medieval castles in Scotland, the castle is an excellent example of the military architecture of this period and lies west of Dunblane at the head of the Trossachs trail.

Dunblane Cathedral

Founded in the 13th century on a hill overlooking the Allan Waters, the cathedral although partly ruined for some time, is now fully restored and has some magnificent stained glass windows.

National Wallace Monument

BELOW On the opposite side of the north/south crossing, below Stirling Castle is the William Wallace monument. Erected above the plain where he won his most triumphant victory against the forces of Edward I at the battle of Stirling Bridge in 1297.

Bannockburn Heritage Centre

ABOVE In June 1314 King Robert the Bruce, routed the English forces on the battlefield of Bannockburn just below Stirling Castle, winning freedom for the Scots. The striking statue of Bruce astride his horse was created by Pilkington Jackson.

Stirling Castle

Like Edinburgh, the rocky volcanic mound at Stirling provided a natural location on which to build a fortification. Dating back to at least 1124 but probably much earlier, the main castle as seen today was largely built in the 16th century to guard the strategic north/south crossing point. Mary, Queen of Scots' was crowned here in 1543.

BELOW *After the betrayal of William Wallace, Robert the Bruce picked up the banner and eventually defeated the army of Edward II at Bannockburn in 1314 gaining independence for Scotland and becoming King.*

87

The Falkirk Wheel

ABOVE *Linking Glasgow to Edinburgh, a total of 11 locks were needed to breach the 85ft (26m) height from the Union canal down to the Forth & Clyde canal at their crossing place in Falkirk. The largest canal restoration project in Britain's history, the ingenious Falkirk Wheel now traverses the locks in one giant rotating step in 15 minutes and is the only rotating boatlift in the world.*

Culross High Street

ABOVE Bypassed by two centuries, many of the buildings in Culross have remained unchanged and offer a wonderful insight into a 17th century village. The cobbled streets of this picturesque Royal Borough take you to the 16th century Palace which dominates the town.

Culross Palace

Kellie Castle, Pittenween

LEFT Dating from 1360, Kellie castle has three adjoining towers, with the oldest 14th century tower having the four circular corner turrets.

Pittenweem

ABOVE Pittenweem, meaning "the place of the cave" is the busiest fishing community along this coastline. Nearby at St Fillan's cave is the 7th century sanctuary of St Fillan after which the village was named. Originally renowned for trading in herring, the main catch today is white fish.

Crail

BELOW Nestled at the end of a steep narrow lane in the East Neuk of Fife lies the picturesque fishing harbour of Crail. Once used by smugglers the harbour is now predominantly a base for lobster and crab fishermen.

St Andrews Castle

This 13/14th century castle is renowned for its siege works and its 24ft (7m) deep bottle dungeon hollowed out of rock. A group of Protestants including John Knox were besieged in the castle for nearly a year, before being captured. The castle can be accessed by a tunnel cut from the outside by the Earl of Arran's men which meets up with a tunnel cut from the inside by the defenders.

John Knox was married in St Andrews Abbey and though it is now a ruin, it was at one time the largest abbey in Scotland. The town is also celebrated as the birthplace of golf.

RRS Discovery

INSET Docked at Dundee's Discovery Point, RRS Discovery was one of the last wooden three-masted ships to be built in Britain, and the first to be built specifically for scientific research. Constructed in Dundee due to its experience of building whaling ships, and launched in 1901, Captain Scott successfully sailed her through icy waters to explore Antarctica.

95

Scone Palace

Built in 1580, the 3rd earl of Mansfield heavily modernised the palace using the existing footprint in 1802. Scone was of great importance to the Picts in the 6th century and is where ancient kings including Robert the Bruce and Macbeth were crowned on the Stone of Destiny. The stone was removed by Edward 1 in 1296 and taken to Westminster Abbey. The stone has now been returned and is retained in Edinburgh Castle.

Branklyn Garden-Perth

INSET One of the finest gardens in Scotland, Branklyn Garden is very well known for its rare and unusual collection of plants, particularly for the rare Himalayan Poppies.

Aberfeldy Birks

The crashing waters and serene woodlands of the Birks of Aberfeldy were immortalised by Robert Burns in his poem of the same name. The walk through the birchwoods up to the falls (particularly in autumn) is inspirational.

Aberfeldy Oatmeal Watermill

Sitting on the Birks of Aberfeldy is the beautifully restored watermill. Originally built in 1825 to process the local grain which grows in this fertile part of Scotland. Today the mill is still in full working order and continues to produce what was once the staple diet in Scotland, ground oatmeal.

Castle Menzies

As home to the Chief of the Clan Menzies until 1918, the castle was built in the 1570's as a "z" plan castle to replace the previous one destroyed by fire. Distinctive with its four round corner turrets, and built from local stone, it has been significantly restored during the past few decades.

Loch Tay

The source of Scotland's most famous salmon river, Loch Tay is one of Scotland's largest lochs and is surrounded by some of the highest mountains in the country.

The Queen's View
Loch Tummel

Killiecrankie

This glorious gorge with the River Garry running through it was not always quite so peaceful . Back in 1689 the first shots were fired in the Jacobite cause. Although the Highlanders won this battle, their heroic leader Bonnie Dundee lost his life here early in the fight. While trying to escape from the Jacobites, one of the English soldiers is believed to have jumped 19ft (6m) across the ragged gorge to his safety.

Blair Athol Distillery

Situated within the picturesque village of Pitlochry, Blair Athol Distillery dating from 1798 offers a traditional distillery experience. The vibrant autumnal leaves stand out in stark contrast to the blackened distillery walls and surrounding trees. The black, soot-like substance is a fungus that thrives on the high alcoholic vapors escaping from the maturing casks.

Blair Castle

RIGHT *The Comyn tower from which the castle has been extended many times dates back to the early 13th century. The last castle in Britain to be sieged, it is the ancestral seat of the Duke of Atholl who keeps the only private army in Europe - the Atholl Highlanders.*

Edradour Distillery

This is Scotland's smallest distillery in full production. What it produces in a year, the larger operations can produce in a week. Being so small, it offers a greater insight into how distilleries would have operated hundreds of years ago as small family business's endeavoring to supplement their incomes as farmers.

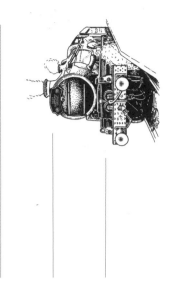

WSR14

WILLITON STATION, THE WEST SOMERSET RAILWAY.

Glamis Castle

A royal residence since 1372 it was the childhood home of H.M. The Queen Mother and the legendary setting of Shakespeare's Macbeth. Originally a simple tower house, its appearance was much enhanced in the 17th century by the addition of two substantial wings and a profusion of turrets.

House of Dun

INSET Surrounded by fine park land and overlooking the Montrose Basin, House of Dun is a beautiful example of a Georgian house. Designed by William Adam in 1730. Although the exterior has a restrained tone, inside the mansion is very sumptuous and displays some amazing plasterwork.

Braemar Castle

ABOVE *Rebuilt in 1748 as a tower house to replace the previous castle built some 100 years earlier. The primary purpose for the castle was to enable the Earl of Mar to exert his authority over his subjects and the neighbouring factions after the Second Jacobite Uprising of 1745. Around the base of the castle is an eight pointed star shaped wall.*

Balmoral Castle

BELOW *The original tower was built in the 15th century. Bought by Prince Albert in 1852, he subsequently had it greatly extended using local granite, into a neo-Gothic castellated mansion for Queen Victoria. The castle has been the holiday home for the Royals ever since.*

The Old Bridge of Dee

The River Dee starts in the Grampian Mountains at Braemar and flows to the sea at Aberdeen. The Old Bridge of Dee lies between Braemar and Balmoral where the majestic Lochnagar in beautiful Royal Deeside can be seen towering in the distance.

Crathes Castle, Banchory

LEFT *Taking some 40 years to build Crathes Castle is a beautiful example of a 16th century castle or tower house, with its "fairytale" turrets which served more as decorative attractions rather than defensive features.*

Drum Castle

ABOVE *The huge square tower of Drum Castle with its 12ft (4m) thick walls, dates back to 13th century and is believed to be one of the oldest tower houses in Scotland. The chapel and adjoining building dates from the 16th century.*

Craigievar Castle

LEFT *One of Scotland's best Baronial Castles, Craigievar was built on a hill side in 1626. With its clutter of turrets, cupolas and corbelling, the castle has taken on a fairytale appearance.*

Castle Fraser

ABOVE *Built between 1575-1636 around an earlier keep, Castle Fraser is considered one of the grandest Castles of Mar and the most elaborate Z-plan castle in Scotland having had little use for its defences.*

Dunnottar Castle - Stonehaven

An imposing fortress site on a spectacular rocky headland, Dunnottar Castle was the last Scottish stronghold to stand against Cromwell's English troops and was the "safe house" for the crown jewels of Scotland from 1651-1652. The castle chapel dates back to the 13th century and the keep from the 14th. The castle was the seat of the Earls of Keith until it was forfeited for their part in the Jacobean uprising.

Stonehaven

INSET A small town south of Aberdeen, Stonehaven's sheltered bay guaranteed its development as a fishing port. Now only a few boats can be seen landing their catch in its picturesque harbour.

Aberdeen

The capital city of North East Scotland,
Aberdeen has many fine buildings of
historic interest including King's College
founded in 1495 (below) and St Machar
Cathedral dating back to the 14th century
(opposite). In the city centre is Provost
Ross's house which was built in 1593 and
is now part of the Aberdeen Maritime
Museum which gives a wonderful insight
into the strong association the city has had
with the sea. The economy of Aberdeen
continues to be dependent on the sea as a
source of fish and oil. In fact it is
considered to be the oil capital of Europe.

RIGHT *Oil supply vessel docks in Aberdeen
harbour.*

LEFT *St Machar's Cathedral*

BELOW *King's College Chapel*

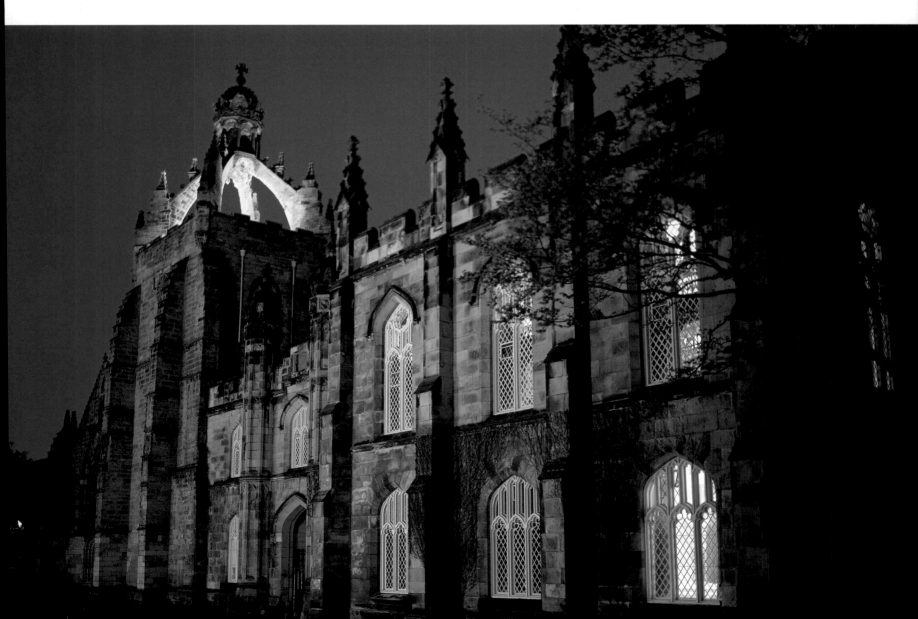

Fyvie Castle

Fyvie Castle dates from the 13th century and boasts five magnificent Baronial towers which were added by five successive lairds. It is also renowned for its great stone wheel stair 13ft (4m) wide, believed to be the finest of its kind in Scotland.

Pitmedden Garden

Re modelled in the 1950's the formal garden consists of four parterres. One parterre is based on the coat-of-arms of Sir Alexander Seton. The other three are believed to be taken from a design used at the Palace of Holyroodhouse c1647.

Fraserburgh Lighthouse Museum

BELOW *Originally a small 16th century castle, the Northern Lighthouse Company changed it into their very first lighthouse in 1787. Although still in perfect working order, it is no longer used to warn ships away from Fraserborough's North-easterly point.*

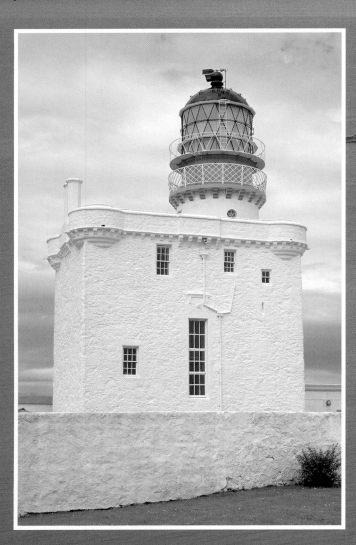

Haddo House

BELOW *Acclaimed as the most elegant Georgian mansion in North East Scotland, Haddo House, built in 1732, portrays the style of William Adam.*

Crovie

With better access to the sea than land, there is no road through the remote village of 40 or so homes. The houses are built gable ends to the sea, in order to withstand the severe weather.

Kildrummy Castle

LEFT *Incorporating a chapel this is one of Scotland's finest 13th century castle ruins, and was at one time one of the most important. Significant as the place where the 1715 Jacobite rising was planned, it was abandoned the following year after the cause failed and the Earl of Mar fled to France.*

Pennan

LEFT A very steep descent down a coastal cliff leads to the famed village of Pennan. Its picturesque position has made it an ideal location for film crews, most notably in the filming of "Local Hero".

Duff House - Banff

BELOW Home to a fine collection of art for the National Galleries of Scotland, Duff House is a splendid example of an early Georgian mansion built at the mouth of the River Deveron.

Huntly Castle

*Built by the powerful Gordons and dating
from the 16th century, Huntly castle still
retains much of its fine masonry work
including the 33ft (10m) heraldic
doorway, inscribed stone friezes and
sculptures.*

Strathisla Distillery

Founded in 1786, Strathisla is the oldest continuously operating distillery in Scotland. In a beautiful location to the east of Keith, it is considered a Speyside whisky, and home of the world famous Chivas Regal brand. Its twin kiln pagodas and waterwheel make it probably the most attractive of all distilleries.

Elgin Cathedral

LEFT Founded in 1224, Elgin Cathedral was sometimes called the Lantern of the North. Now mostly in ruin, it was said to have been one of the most attractive cathedrals ever built. Despite this it was destroyed in 1390 by the Wolf of Badenoch.

Pluscarden Abbey - Elgin

BELOW Founded in 1230 by Alexander II. The abbey fell into disarray after the time of the reformation, but restoration began in the 19th century by the Marquiss of Bute. The rebuilding was continued by the monks who moved back in 1948. Making it one of the finest in Scotland.

The Glenlivet Distillery

One of the best known Scotch whiskies, Glenlivet has built on a reputation established almost 200 years ago. The first licensed distiller in 1824, Glenlivet has led the way ever since with many neighbouring distillers attaching the name Glenlivet to their produce. Glenlivet eventually won the exclusive right to brand their whisky "The Glenlivet".

Ballindalloch Castle

INSET Situated in beautiful grounds in the heart of Speyside's whisky country, Ballindalloch Castle is privately owned and has been the home of the Macpherson-Grants since 1546 from which time the prominent central tower also dates.

Brodie Castle

Dating from the 16th century, Brodie is a Z-plan tower house. Following a major attack in 1645 by Montros's army the castle was extended in the 17th and 19th centuries. Through the spring, the gardens bloom with daffodils.

Spey River

Stretching from the south of Aviemore to the Moray Firth just east of Elgin, the Spey is Britain's fastest flowing river and is the main artery through Speyside. As the life line for salmon and trout, it is also the life line for many communities which have built up along it's banks. In particular the river feeds Scotland's premier and largest whisky producing region. Although few use the water directly from the Spey, over 40 distilleries obtain their water from springs and burns which feed into the Spey.

133

Cawdor Castle

Although this is one of Scotland's oldest tower houses, with the central keep dating back to the 14th century, it clearly does not date back to the time of Macbeth in 1040 with which it has become synonymous. Nevertheless the notoriety gained from Shakespeare's Scottish tragedy has played a part in Cawdor acquiring the title "the most romantic castle in the Highlands".

Fort George

RIGHT *Built after the battle of Culloden to intimidate the demoralised Jocobites, this substantial and heavily defended fortification has never actually seen a shot fired in anger.*

Inverness Castle

Built on the site of the original Fort George which was destroyed by the Jacobites in 1746, the existing castle was built in 1830. With its obvious strategic position defensive fortifications have been built on the site going back to the 12th century.

Suenos Stone

ABOVE *The Suenos Stone is 23ft (7m) high and is the most outstanding of the various standing stones in the Moray area. Although these stones record the presence of the Picts who inhabited Scotland prior to the Scots, the meaning of the inscriptions is unclear. The two pervading theories being the recording of great battles or as monuments to heroic leaders.*

Carrbridge

LEFT *Dating back to 1717 the precarious looking bridge at Carrbridge spans the River Dulnain and was built to provide safer access to the village. Its design has enabled it to survive almost three centuries.*

Culloden Moor

ABOVE/RIGHT *On a bleak day in April 1746 Culloden Moor became the site of the last major battle on British soil. Outnumbered by the Duke of Cumberland's government troops, Prince Charles Edward Stuart led his Jacobite Rising into a courageous but devastating defeat which was to be the end of his hopes to regain the British throne.*

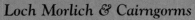

Loch Morlich & Cairngorms

Four of the highest mountains in Britain form part of the glacial landscape region known as the Cairngorms. The highest peak in the range and second highest in Scotland is Ben Macdui at 4,295 ft (1309 m). Nestling below the Cairngorms is Loch Morlich which offers fine views of this mountain wilderness.

Loch Garten Osprey Centre

LEFT *Situated within the Abernethy Forest Nature Reserve, owned by the RSPB, Loch Garten is the home to many rare species of birds and wildlife. For many visitors catching sight of a fishing Osprey is the highlight.*

Loch an Eilein (castle), Aviemore

Situated on the Rothiemurchus Estate, within the ancient Caledonian Forests the 13th century Island Castle ruin was reputed to have been a stronghold of the "Wolf of Badenoch"!
The Cairngorm Mountains can be seen in the distance.

Cairngorm Mountains

The Cairngorm Mountains are made up of Granite rock and is the largest continuous area of ground above 3000ft (1,000m) in Britain. The mountain railway whisks visitors up Cairn Gorm in just 8 minutes to a magnificent viewpoint just below the summit. Cairn Gorm is 4,085ft (1245m) and on a clear day Ben Nevis can be seen in the distance.

Cairngorm Ski Area

Scotland's premier Ski resort is built around a sub artic bowl which retains the snow in the winter. At over 3000ft (1,000m) this is an ideal place for skiers of any ability or for people just wishing to enjoy the panoramic views.

Dalwhinnie Distillery

Considered a Highland Malt, Dalwhinnie is believed to be the highest Distillery in Scotland and stands at the junction of a major whisky smuggling route. Its single malt is made from snow melt water and makes an excellent introduction for would be connoisseurs.

Loch Ness

Loch Ness is the largest body of fresh water in Britain. It is 23 miles (37km) long and over 750ft (230m) deep, consequently it is easy to appreciate how people can believe something could be hiding in its depths.

Glen Affric

INSET Considered one of Scotland's most beautiful glens, Glen Affric lies west of Loch Ness but is much quieter and more peaceful. The ancient Caledonian pine-clad glen incorporates two stunning lochs fed by the river Affric.

Loch Ness, Urquhart Castle

At 23 miles long, over 750ft (229m) deep and part of the Great Glen, Loch Ness is a huge body of water. Once visited, it is understandable that it has maintained its mystery of an illusive creature since 565 AD. Urquhart Castle, dates back to the 13th century and was one of Scotland's largest castles until it was largely destroyed by government troops in 1692. The prominent tower house, although in ruin still offers tremendous views up and down the loch.

Glen Nevis-Ben Nevis

At 4,406ft (1,344m) high, Ben Nevis is Britain's highest mountain. Although only the peak is visible when viewed from the western side, Glen Nevis - "The Grandest Mile in Britain" provides hikers access up the mountain past the 350ft (107m) magnificent Steall Waterfall.

Glenfinnan Monument over Loch Shiel

INSET Erected in 1815 at the head of Loch Shiel to commenmorate where the clans gathered to support Bonnie Prince Charlie's 1745 Jacobite Rebellion.

Kintail, Glen Shiel

ABOVE/RIGHT *Having marched approximately 10 miles from Eilean Donan Castle, a 300 strong force of Jacobite and Spanish soldiers were eventually held back by Cumberland's army along Kintail and sent into retreat. An arduous hike leads to the Falls of Glomach. At 350ft (107m) deep, they are considered to be the most spectacular in Britain.*

Eilean Donan Castle

LEFT *Acclaimed the most romantic castle in Scotland, it was originally built in 1220 on a rocky tidal island in Loch Duich. The scene of a Jacobite battle in 1719, it was virtually destroyed under heavy attack from English warships. It remained a ruin until 1912 when a 28 year restoration programme began which brought the castle back to its present appearance. It has since been used in a number of films including `Highlander`. A causeway bridge provides access from the mainland.*

153

Skye

Cuillin Hills from Loch Slapin

Providing some of Europe's most challenging climbs, the Cuillins incorporate 11 Munros with the highest being Sgurr Alasdair at 1009m (3,310ft)

Armadale Castle

INSET *The Clan MacDonald arrived on Skye in the mid 15th century, eventually some of the clan chiefs took up residence in Armdale in the 1650's. 100 years on, Flora MacDonald was married here in 1750, then in 1815 the mansion house was extended to form Armdale Castle. Much of this was destroyed by fire in 1855 and subsequently rebuilt.*

Skye

The Quiraing

The pinnacles of the Quairing is just one of the unusual rock formations which form part of the 20 mile long Trotternish Ridge, the longest land slip in Britain.

Neist Point

Stretching out to sea, windswept and remote the light house at the end of the 300 ft cliffs which form Neist Point, marks the most westerly point on Skye.

Skye

Kilt Rock

Kilt Rock is formed from alternating bands of hard and soft rock resulting in a series of circular and stripped rock formations with the appearance of pleated kilts.

Dunvegan Castle

Standing on the western shore of Skye is Dunvegan Castle, which has been home to the Chiefs of Clan MacLeods continuously since the 13th century. Originally the only access was via the sea gate when it was built as a keep.

Skye

The Cuillins from Loch Harport

Dominating the south of the island the Cuillins form a serrated ridge over eight miles long.

Lewis -
Outer Hebrides

Callanish Standing Stones

Believed to be marking certain points during the lunar calendar, the Callanish Standing Stones form a series of circles and avenues using over 50 standing stones with the central stone standing over 14ft (4.5m) high. 5000 years old the monument was virtually hidden under peat until it was excavated in 1857.

North Uist -
Outer Hebrides

Crofters Cottage

BELOW A typical thatch roofed croft
standing over one of the many beautiful
and remote sandy beaches along North
Uist's western coastline.

Barra -
Outer Hebrides

Kisimul Castle

A sea fortress has stood on this rock in the
middle of Caste Bay since the 1040's.
With two wells and a fish trap, the
stronghold of Clan MacNeill was well
equipped to withstand the longest siege.

Bealach-na-Ba, Applecross

BELOW A narrow road threads its way up over the 2,000ft (610m) pass of Bealach na Ba (the pass of the cattle) to Applecross with terrific views in all directions. Until 1970 this was the only road to Applecross making it very isolated during the winter months.

Loch Torridon

Loch Torridon is a sea loch which shimmers in turquoise blue and is best viewed from the road along its southern shore. Beinn Alligin is the peak seen to the left of the picture and marks the western end of the Torridon mountain range, while 3,456ft (1,054m) Liathach stands over the tiny village huddled along the loch shore.

Torridon

Forming the most northerly range of Highland mountains is the Moine Trust. Travelling 100 miles north it encompasses the magnificent Torridon mountains which boasts six peaks over 3,000ft (914m) and offers spectacular scenery and more solitude than many of the more southerly mountain ranges.

Loch Diabaig

INSET Framed by steeply sided rocky terrain, remote Loch Diabaig is an offshoot of Loch Torridon, eight miles along its northern shoreline.

Loch Maree

LEFT *Part of Britain's first National Nature Reserve, the loch and its islands scattered with oaks and Caledonian pines are now protected under the Scottish Natural Heritage. The main Isle was once a sacred place for druids.*

Inverewe Garden

BELOW *Set in a location as stunning as the gardens, Inverewe lies on a peninsula along Loch Ewe on Scotland's North West coast. Benefiting from the warm air of the Gulf Stream, the garden boasts a diverse collection of plants from both Northern and Southern hemispheres.*

Loch Maree/Slioch
The imposing 3,217ft (980m) peak of Slioch stands on the Eastern side of Loch Maree in Glen Docherty.

Red Deer Stag
The Red Deer is Britain's largest land mammal.

Quinag, Loch Assynt

Quinag is a formidable mountain massif.
Made of red Torridonian sandstone its
highest peak is 2,650ft (808m).

Beinn Dearg, Loch Glascarnoch

LEFT *Beinn Dearg means 'Red Hill'. At 3,556ft (1084m) it is the most prominent mountain in its range.*

175

Glenmorangie Distillery

With a worldwide reputation and highly regarded among the Scots, Glenmorangie has been distilling whisky since 1843 from this very location and no doubt illegally before that. A tour inside reveals its unique tall slender necked stills ensuring only the lightest spirit is used.

Falls of Rogie

FAR RIGHT The 44ft (13m) staggered Falls of Rogie offer the opportunity to see salmon forge their way up the Black Water River. This is also a peaceful and spectacularly beautiful area, which is worth the short hike.

176

Courthouse & Hugh Millers Cottage, Cromarty

Nestling within the once prosperous fishing village of Cromarty are the 18th century Courthouse and Cottage of Hugh Miller. The Courthouse is now a museum where visitors can see an 18th century trial re-enacted. Close by is Hugh Miller's thatched roof cottage which displays numerous artefacts of Scotland's most notable geologist. The house was built with small windows and gable end to the sea to withstand the harsh coastal conditions. It is one of the most northerly thatched cottages in Britain.

Loch Fleet

BELOW An east coast sea loch, this Scottish Wildlife Trust reserve is home to seals as well as many rare birds.

Shin Falls

LEFT *Salmon swimming upstream from the North Sea to Loch Shin can be seen leaping up the falls as they head back to their spawning grounds.*

Loch Shin

The largest loch in Sutherland, Loch Shin is over 17 miles (27 km) long and feeds the river Shin and Shin Falls, famed for their abundance of salmon and trout.

Dunrobin Castle

This huge white multi-sided "fairytale" castle was built over many centuries. In part, it dates back to the 13th century but with three additions in the 17th, 18th and 19th century's it became the largest house in the North Highlands.

**Duncansby Head
John O'Groats**

INSET *The north-eastern point of mainland
Scotland is Dunscansby Head. Its 250ft
(76m) high leaning cliffs are the windy
home to huge flocks of nesting birds. On a
clear day Orkney can be seen from this
point.*

**Duncansby Stacks
John O'Groats**

*A short walk from Duncansby Head leads
to the Stacks which are three precarious
rocky outcrops left standing proud as the
sea mercilessly erodes the sandstone cliffs.*

184

Orkney Islands

Skara Brae

LEFT *Covered by sand dunes for thousands of years until an Atlantic storm exposed it in 1850, Skara Brae is one of the best preserved Stone Age settlements in Western Europe. Great detail of the interior remains, including jewellery, hearths, beds and other items of stone furniture from Neolithic times.*

Broch of Gurness

RIGHT *One of the best preserved brochs on Orkney, the Broch of Gurness is surrounded by Iron Age buildings and is calculated to date from the 1st century.*

Ring of Brogar

BELOW *These mysterious standing stones, some standing 4.5m high, are believed to have been erected in 2800 BC. Of the original 60 stones in the circle, 36 are still erect after nearly 5,000 years.*

Orkney Islands

St Magnus Cathedral

Founded in the 12th century with vibrant yellow and red sandstone, taking 300 years to complete and incorporates many transitional styles of building including Gothic and Romanesque. Two skeletons, one of which is believed to be that of St Magnus were discovered in one of the pillars

Highland Park Distillery

Established in 1798, Highland Park is Scotlands most northerly distillery. Highland Park Whisky is still produced by traditional methods giving it a unique character. This is one of only a few distilleries that still fires the kilns with locally cut peat and malts barley on its malting floor.

Italian Chapel

Built around two corrugated iron Nissen Huts and decorated with salvaged materials in 1943 by Italian prisoners of the second world war who had been taken here to help build the Churchill Barriers blocking German U Boats from entering Scapa Flow and attacking British warships.

Shetland

Clickhimin Broch
A beautifully simple and symmetrical broch, its location close to a sea loch and surrounded by marshland is an obvious choice. Clickhimin Broch was built within an Iron Age fort and dates back some 2,500 years.

Jarlshof
BELOW *The site of Jarlshof has been used as a strategic settlement since the Bronze Age and through to medieval times. An Iron Age broch has been built over the top of numerous Bronze Age buildings including a smiddy. Picts, Vikings and Medieval homesteaders have left their mark, although the greatest mark left on the site is the ruined 16th century house of the Stewart Earls.*

Scalloway Castle
Built with forced labour by the tyrannical
Earl Patrick Stewart, Scalloway was built
in 1600, although the Earl did not have
long to enjoy his new home, being
executed in 1615 for his cruelty and
extortion of his people.

Index